SIKH BELIEFS AND ISSUES

Michael Keene

Badger
Publishing

CONTENTS

WHO ARE THE SIKHS?

Sikhism is the youngest of the major world religions. It was born around the end of the 15th century, in an area of what is now Pakistan and north-west India called the **Punjab**. At that time, the Punjab was ruled over by Muslims.

BEGINNINGS

The founder of Sikhism was **Guru Nanak**, who was born a Hindu. He did not, however, grow up to follow the Hindu religion, although he kept a warm affection for it in his heart. Guru Nanak disagreed with many of its beliefs and ways of worshipping.

Guru Nanak taught a small group of followers that there is only one God and that all people, of whatever religion, are equal in God's sight. These remain the basic beliefs of Sikhism.

WHAT IS A SIKH?

Originally the word 'Sikh' simply meant a 'disciple'. A meeting held at **Amritsar** in 1931 defined a true Sikh as someone who:

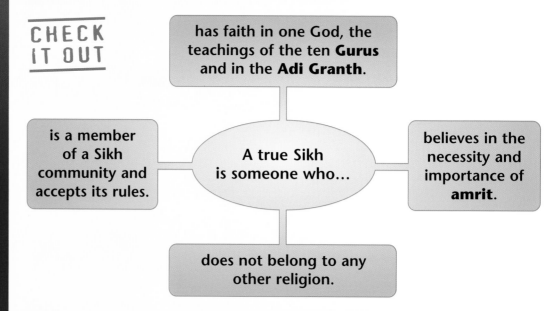

CHECK IT OUT

has faith in one God, the teachings of the ten **Gurus** and in the **Adi Granth**.

is a member of a Sikh community and accepts its rules.

A true Sikh is someone who...

believes in the necessity and importance of **amrit**.

does not belong to any other religion.

THE IMPORTANCE OF PERSONAL HYGIENE

Although Sikhs are to be found throughout the world, the faith belongs firmly to the Indian religious tradition. This tradition stresses the importance of personal appearance and hygiene. As part of this, Sikhs wear a **turban** and the **Five Ks** [Units 8 and 9]. These are the visible expressions of the Sikh faith.

To underline the importance of hygiene, all Sikh acts of worship are preceded by bathing. This expresses the Sikh belief that only those who are physically clean can enter the presence of God.

When Sikhs enter a **gurdwara** [Unit 12], they take off their shoes as a mark of respect to God. God's presence is symbolised by the holy book – the **Guru Granth Sahib** – which is also known as the Adi Granth. Even to carry one's shoes through the gurdwara is an insult to the holy book.

Wherever in the world Sikhs are found, they form a gurdwara so that the Guru Granth Sahib has a home.

WHERE ARE SIKHS FOUND?

There are about 20 million Sikhs in the world today. Most of them live in the Punjab and the surrounding states. About 1 million live elsewhere in the world with:

- 400,000 living in the UK
- 300,000 living in Canada
- 100,000 living in the USA

and the rest are scattered throughout Europe, Australia, Africa and East Asia.

OVER TO YOU ▶▶▶

1 The Sikh name for their place of worship – the gurdwara – means 'an open door'. Why do you think this is a very good name for a place of worship?

2 The map on this page shows the Indian state of Punjab, which is where most of the world's Sikhs live. Try to find out as much as you can about this part of India. In particular, find out what happened in the Punjab in 1947.

TAKE TIME TO THINK

In many religions, the cleanliness of the body is stressed almost as much as spiritual preparation before worship. Why do you think it is thought to be so important?

AFGHANISTAN

CHINA

• Amritsar

Punjab

PAKISTAN

Himalayas

• Delhi

NEPAL

INDIA

The Punjab – the part of the world that is the home to most of the world's Sikhs.

GURU NANAK – THE EARLY YEARS

The 'land of the five rivers' in north India has always been known as the Punjab. This is a very fertile area where much of India's food is grown. For this reason, ancient rulers always wanted to own the land. It also straddled the old trade routes which began in Europe and passed through India on the way to the East. This made it very valuable.

As the traders moved around, so they took different beliefs about God and ways of worshipping with them. The old faith of Hinduism and the much newer faith of Islam were particularly important. Islam was the main religious faith of the rulers of parts of north India between the 14th and 17th centuries CE.

THE YOUNG GURU NANAK

Guru Nanak was born in 1469 in Talwindi [now called Nankana Sahib], which is a small town about 50 miles to the south-west of Lahore, in modern Pakistan. He belonged to a reasonably prosperous Hindu family. Nanak was the first of ten Gurus who founded the Sikh religion.

There are many unusual events connected with his childhood:

CHECK IT OUT

Unusual events associated with Guru Nanak

On one occasion, he spent the money his father had given him to help the poor rather than using it to trade.

A normally deadly cobra shaded his face from the sun.

On one occasion, he allowed his cattle to graze on a neighbouring farm. When the neighbour complained, he found his field untouched.

Guru Nanak denied that he could perform miracles – except in God's name. He once said:

A **"***Mighty is the Lord and great His gifts.***"**

In those days, people married young and Nanak was only about 16 when he married. His father arranged who he should marry. This was the custom in those days and still is in many Hindu families. When his first son was born, however, he refused to carry out the usual Hindu ceremonies. Birth, he said, is a natural event and the only impurity is:

B **"***…the covetous mind, tongues speaking untruths, eyes full of lust and ears accepting unreliable evidence as true.***"**

In saying this, he was denying the Hindu teaching that everyone is born sinful because of bad **karma** from a previous existence.

For 14 years, Nanak served the provincial governor as a storekeeper but gradually an interest in spiritual matters began to take over. He spent most of his leisure time in meditation and solitude.

This wall-covering shows the first of the Sikh Gurus, Guru Nanak, and the last, **Guru Gobind Singh**.

OVER TO **YOU** ▶▶▶

1 Why was the Punjab such an important area in ancient times over which many battles were fought?

2 Write up a description of the early life of Guru Nanak suitable to be published in your local paper, pointing out in your article why the young child was thought to be an unusual child.

3 It seems that the birth of religious leaders often have miracles and supernatural events attached to them. Describe one leader other than Guru Nanak of whom this could be said – and describe one such event.

TAKE TIME TO THINK

What do you think that Guru Nanak meant when he said the only impurity is "the covetous mind, tongues speaking untruths, eyes full of lust and ears accepting unreliable evidence as true"?

GURU NANAK'S SPIRITUAL EXPERIENCE

You will find out

- About Guru Nanak's visit to the Courts of Heaven.

- What Guru Nanak did after returning to Earth.

- The message that Guru Nanak preached to the people.

In the glossary

Amrit

Gurdwara

Guru

Guru Nanak

Karah Parshad

Punjab

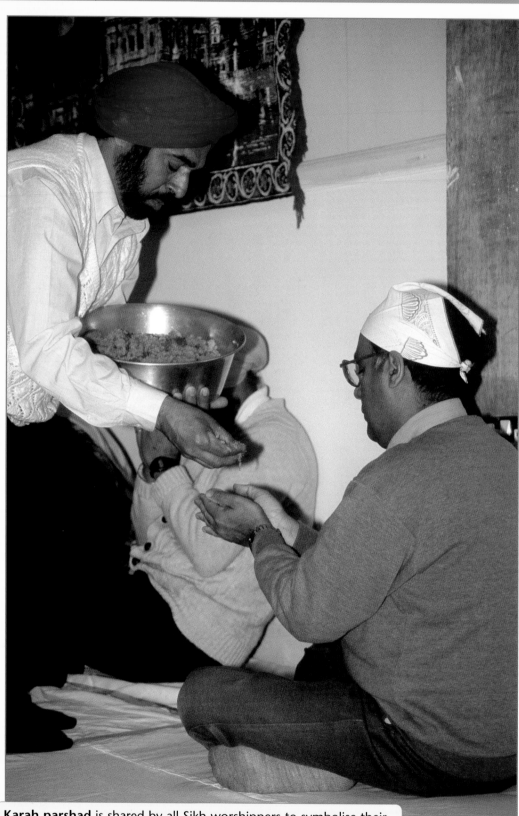

Karah parshad is shared by all Sikh worshippers to symbolise their unity with each other, just as amrit symbolises their unity with God.

After spending many years meditating on the name of God and praying, Guru Nanak had a remarkable spiritual experience when he was thirty years old. This experience changed the whole direction of his life:

GURU NANAK VISITS THE COURTS OF HEAVEN

Guru Nanak was bathing in the River Bein, near Sultanpur, when he suddenly felt himself being taken up to the divine court to appear in the presence of God. You can read in Extract A how he described this experience:

A *"I was a minstrel out of work. The Lord gave me employment. The Mighty One instructed me, 'Night and day, sing my praise'. The Lord summoned the minstrel to his High Court. On me he bestowed the robe of honouring him and singing his praise. On me he bestowed the nectar in a cup, the nectar of his true and holy name."*

Then:

- He was given a cup of nectar [amrit] to drink.
- God spoke to him.
- He returned to Earth after three days away, where he found that the people were convinced that he had drowned.
- He remained silent for another day before telling the people the message that he had been given. [B] He told the people that God had called him to be a 'guru' or spiritual teacher.

B *"There is neither Hindu nor Muslim so whose path shall I follow? I shall follow God's path. God is neither Hindu nor Muslim and the path which I follow is God's."*

For the next twenty years, Guru Nanak travelled through India and the adjoining Muslim countries, visiting all the holy places of Hinduism and Islam and talking to their religious leaders. Then, in later life, he settled down as a farmer in the Punjab with his family. Gradually, a community of followers grew up around him. A few days before his death, in 1539, Guru Nanak nominated his most faithful disciple to succeed him.

THE MESSAGE OF GURU NANAK

The message that Guru Nanak, preached to the people was very clear and, in many ways, it cut across their Hindu and Muslim beliefs. He told them that:

- There is one God who is both present with them in the world and yet over and above that world.
- There is a continual cycle of birth, death and rebirth.
- The goal of every person's soul is to finally be absorbed into God.
- Those who hope to be absorbed into God must discipline themselves and live their lives according to certain moral principles.
- Above everything else, people must live their lives in humility at the service of others.

OVER TO YOU ▶▶▶

Look at Extract A.

1 Who was this "minstrel" and why was this name appropriate for him?
2 How did the Lord summon the minstrel to the High Court?
3 What was the nectar that the minstrel drank?
4 How did the minstrel set out to honour God?

TAKE TIME TO THINK

What do you think Guru Nanak is trying to say in Extract B and why do you think this was such an unusual message?

THE LATER GURUS

Sikhs believe that they need guidance from a Guru to reach God. The word itself comes from a Sanskrit word meaning 'heavy', meaning that a Guru teaches heavy or weighty matters about God. After the death of Guru Nanak, there were nine other human Gurus:

GURU ANGAD [1539-52]

Guru Nanak's faithful follower, Lehna, was appointed by Nanak to succeed him. He created a special language in which the Sikh scriptures could be written, called **Gurmukhi**. This gave the Sikh community a special identity. He also wrote many hymns that are included in the Guru Granth Sahib.

GURU AMAR DAS [1552-74]

It was Guru Amar Das, the third Guru, who created the open kitchen, the **langar**, which is to be found in every gurdwara. He did it so that anyone could sit with him in discussion or worship.

GURU RAM DAS [1574-81]

Guru Ram Das founded the holy city of **Amritsar**. He also wrote the hymn that is performed at all Sikh weddings. Until this time, Sikh couples had to go through a Hindu wedding ceremony.

Guru Gobind Singh – the last of the ten Sikh Gurus.

Guru Arjan Dev [1581-1606]

Guru Arjan Dev, the fifth Guru, built the temple, the **Harimandir**, that stands in the middle of a lake in Amritsar. It is known as the **Golden Temple** as it was later covered with gold leaf. He also composed hymns and collected together many written by the other Gurus and published them as 'the first book' – the Adi Granth. These later became a part of the full collection in the Guru Granth Sahib.

Guru Arjan Dev was later put to death for his faith. He died a horrible death. He was roasted alive and his body was thrown in the river.

Guru Har Gobind [1606-1644]

Guru Har Gobind carried two swords – for warfare and to fight for the truth of the spirit. This was the beginning of accepting the use of violence in self-defence in Sikhism. The Sikhs were trained to fight and built a fort at Amritsar.

Guru Har Rai [1644-61]

More violence was directed against the Sikh community and they had to withdraw into the mountains.

Guru Har Krishnan [1661-64]

This Guru was only six years old when he was elected. He set up charitable works to look after smallpox suffers but caught the disease himself and died at the age of seven.

Guru Tegh Bahadur [1664-75]

Fought against the emperor, who wanted him to convert to Islam. He was captured and beheaded. He became the second martyred Guru.

Guru Gobind Rai [Singh] [1675-1708]

The tenth, and last Guru, instituted the **Khalsa** brotherhood and the amrit ceremony – taking the name Singh, as do all men in the Khalsa. He told his followers that there would be no more human Gurus. Instead, the holy book, the Guru Granth Sahib, would be the Guru.

He brought together the Guru Granth Sahib so that it had 31 divisions – each of them beginning with the **Mool Mantra**. So the Adi Granth became 'the revered teacher book', the Guru Granth Sahib.

OVER TO YOU ▶▶▶

1 Write down in a sentence what a guru is.
2 Write down one thing for which each of the later nine Gurus was famous or important.
3 What is the relationship between the Adi Granth and the Guru Granth Sahib?

TAKE TIME TO THINK

Look at the picture of Guru Gobind Singh. Can you see any clues about the kind of person that this Guru was?

UNIT 5
BELIEVING IN GOD

You will find out

- The Sikh belief that God is present in nature.

- The Sikh belief that God is one.

- The Sikh belief that God is everything.

- The importance of God's name in Sikhism.

In the glossary

Guru

Guru Gobind Singh

Guru Granth Sahib

Guru Nanak

Simran

Waheguru

A Sikh's belief in God is the foundation of his or her life. Yet, as the Sikh scriptures constantly teach, no one can reach a complete understanding of God or His creation. Each religion brings its own insights and approaches to God, with all of them being helpful. As Guru Gobind Singh once said:

A **"***Men, according to different understandings, have given different descriptions of thee, O Lord.***"**

Guru Gobind Singh

Sikhs believe that:

GOD IS PRESENT IN NATURE

God is always found in nature and creation. It is the work of holy men and saints to make people aware of this. This was particularly the work of the different Gurus. They were sent to pass God's word on to others. Their revelations are preserved in the Guru Granth Sahib. It is this holy book, more than anything else, that makes God known. As the Guru Granth Sahib says:

B **"***You are clearly present in the world, O Lord, Because all crave your name.***"**

GOD IS ONE

The early followers of Guru Nanak were Hindus. They had been encouraged to worship many gods and goddesses. From the Guru they learned that there is one God and that God alone should be worshipped. His qualities are endless.

GOD IS EVERYTHING

God is everything to the Sikh. He is all-powerful, seeing all things and directing the affairs of His children. He listens to their prayers and gives them all good gifts. God can be reached by all people and each person's soul is a part of God.

CHECK IT OUT

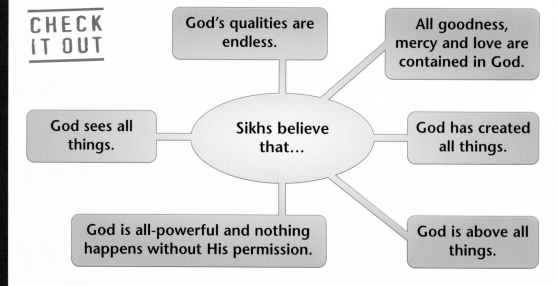

God's qualities are endless.

All goodness, mercy and love are contained in God.

God sees all things.

Sikhs believe that...

God has created all things.

God is all-powerful and nothing happens without His permission.

God is above all things.

This Sikh, like all Sikhs, hopes to keep the name of God in the forefront of his mind always.

GOD'S NAME IS ALL-IMPORTANT

The most important religious activity for every Sikh is **simran** – the calling to mind of God's name and keeping that name always in the forefront of the mind. To do this, he or she must think constantly of God's different qualities – although they are too numerous for any human being to understand fully.

There are two important ways of doing this:

- To learn the scriptures by heart, since they are full of God's glory.

- By repeating one name – **Waheguru** – Wonderful Lord. As the person repeats this name, so they find their soul being drawn closer to God. In this way, they have taken the first step towards salvation.

OVER TO **YOU** ▶▶▶

1 All of the major world religions, apart from Buddhism, teach that there is one God. Can you come up with one reason why they all reject the idea that there might be many gods?

2 The Guru Granth Sahib teaches that God is hidden in every human heart and that every heart is illumined by Him. Do you think that this suggests that the truth of God is only to be found in those who follow the Guru's teachings?

TAKE TIME TO THINK

The Guru Granth Sahib teaches that the True One [God] "is not far from us, but resides in us". What do you think this means?

THE KHALSA

You will find out

- About the Faithful Ones.

- The Code of Discipline which all members of the Khalsa are expected to follow.

In the glossary

Amrit

Guru

Guru Gobind Singh

Khalsa

Khanda

Panj Pyares

During the 17th century, the Muslim rulers of India were forcing Sikhs to convert to Islam. They killed Tegh Bahadur, the 9th Guru, and many of his followers. He was succeeded by the last of the human Gurus – Gobind Rai [known as Gobind Singh].

THE FAITHFUL ONES

As soon as Gobind Rai became Guru, he called all Sikhs together for the April festival of Baisakhi. He asked the large assembly who would be prepared to die for their faith. He made the request with a drawn sword in his hand. Then:

- After a long silence, one man went into the Guru's tent.

- The Guru reappeared with a bloodstained sword.

- Four more men went into the tent.

- The five Faithful Ones [the **Panj Pyares** as they are now called] came out of the tent with the Guru.

All Sikhs today pay their respects to the faith of the five men – the Faithful Ones. The five Faithful Ones formed the nucleus of the Khalsa [the 'Pure Ones']. They were given nectar [amrit] made from water and sugar crystals, which was prepared in an iron bowl and stirred with a double-edged sword [called a **khanda**]. The Guru himself then received the same initiation.

THE CODE OF DISCIPLINE

Guru Gobind Rai laid down a strict code of discipline for those Sikhs who wanted to become members of the Khalsa:

CHECK IT OUT

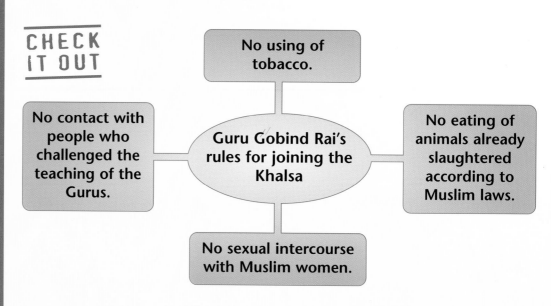

No using of tobacco.

No contact with people who challenged the teaching of the Gurus.

Guru Gobind Rai's rules for joining the Khalsa

No eating of animals already slaughtered according to Muslim laws.

No sexual intercourse with Muslim women.

The first amrit ceremony being conducted by Guru Gobind Singh.

Men who became members of the Khalsa were to take on the surname of 'Singh', meaning 'lion', so that Guru Gobind Rai became Guru Gobind Singh – the name by which he is known. Women were also allowed to become members of the Khalsa and they took the surname 'Kaur', meaning 'princess'.

Soon the number of Sikhs who received their 'baptism by the sword' increased considerably. The Khalsa has remained the focus of the unity between Sikhs ever since. In Unit 7, we will discover how this ceremony is carried out and what it means to the Sikhs who go through it.

OVER TO **YOU** ▶▶▶

1 Write down five pieces of information about the Panj Pyares – the Faithful Ones.

2 Describe, in your own words, the process by which Guru Gobind Singh chose the first five members of the Khalsa.

TAKE TIME TO THINK

Look carefully at the picture on this page. It shows the first amrit ceremony, with two dead hawks lying on their backs while the two doves which have killed them are perched on a bowl of nectar. What do you think this symbolises?

THE AMRIT PAHUL CEREMONY

You will find out

- About the Amrit Pahul ceremony.
- The importance of receiving amrit.
- The requirements of the Khalsa.

In the glossary

Amrit

Amrit-dhari

Amrit Pahul

Ardas

Five Ks

Guru Gobind Singh

Hukam

Japji

Khalsa

Mool Mantra

Panj Pyares

The Amrit Pahul is carried out in private because it is between an individual and God – and no one else.

The **Amrit Pahul** is the most important ceremony in the life of most Sikhs, although not every Sikh goes through it. To those who do, it shows a readiness to be fully committed to their faith. In this ceremony, a person becomes a member of the Khalsa – the Sikh brotherhood. It is open to anyone, male or female, aged sixteen and over, to join.

THE AMRIT PAHUL CEREMONY

This ceremony is similar to that carried out by Guru Gobind Singh when the first five members – the Panj Pyares – were initiated into the Khalsa in 1699. At the Amrit Pahul ceremony, the Panj Pyares are represented by five **amrit-dhari**, Sikhs who have already been through the ceremony. For this they wear the ceremonial saffron dress and the Five Ks.

The ceremony begins with the opening of the scriptures and those wishing to be initiated are asked:

- Are you willing to read, learn and live according to the teachings of Sikhism?
- Will you only pray to the one God?
- Will you serve the whole of humanity?

A prayer is then said and a **hukam** is made from the scriptures.

RECEIVING AMRIT

The five amrit-dhari mix together the ingredients for the amrit during the ceremony.

- For this, they use a double-edged sword and kneel around a bowl.

- The water represents purity. The sugar, as it dissolves, represents the disappearance of all differences between them.

- They say prayers, including the **Japji** and the very important **Ardas** prayer.

- The candidates are baptised by drinking a handful of amrit. They do this five times. Each time they say:

A *"The Khalsa is dedicated to God. The victory belongs to God."*

The Mool Mantra is said five times and the rules of the Khalsa are explained to each person. The ceremony ends with the saying of the Ardas.

REQUIREMENTS OF THE KHALSA

Guru Gobind Singh explained the requirements laid on those who would belong to the Khalsa:

B *"He who repeats day and night the name of God whose enduring light is unquenchable. He who bestows not a thought on any but the one God. He who has full love and confidence in God and who places no faith, even by mistake, in fasting, worshipping at tombs, places of cremation or at places where yogis meditate. He who recognises only the one true God and cares not for pilgrimages, alms, penances and austerities.*

In those hearts the light of the perfect one shines, he is recognised as a pure member of the Khalsa."

Guru Gobind Singh

OVER TO **YOU** ▶▶▶

1 Write a sentence explaining the meaning of:
   a) Amrit-dhari
   b) Hukam
   c) Japji
   d) Ardas

2 Read Extract B.
   a) Several religious activities are mentioned in this extract – and condemned. What are they?
   b) Why do you think that these religious activities are condemned?
   c) How can a pure member of the Khalsa be recognised?

TAKE TIME TO THINK

Can you think of any ceremony in another religion which is designed to show a person's commitment to their faith? Write down all that you remember about this ceremony.

THE KESH, THE KANGHA AND THE KIRPAN

You will find out

- The importance of kesh, long hair, to a Sikh.

- The symbolic importance of the kirpan, the sword.

- The use that Sikhs make of the kangha, the comb.

In the glossary

Five Ks

Guru

Guru Gobind Singh

Kangha

Kesh

Khalsa

Kirpan

Punjab

Turban

Everyone who is a full member of the Khalsa wears five symbols – whether they are men or women. They are known as the Five Ks because, in the Punjabi language, each of them begins with the letter 'K'.

Each of the Five Ks was introduced by Guru Gobind Singh, who explained in a letter:

A *"I am much pleased with you all. You must take the baptism of the sword from five: keep your hair uncut – this is the seal of the Guru. Never be complacent about the pair of shorts and the sword. Always wear on your wrist a steel bracelet, keep your hair neat and clean and comb it twice a day. Always read and recite the hymns of the Guru. Meditate on the name of the Wonderful Lord – God alone. Keep the symbols of the faith as the Guru has told you."*

Three of the Five Ks are:

KESH

Kesh means uncut hair. This is a sign of a Sikh's dedication to God. The hair is bunched up, fixed with a comb [a **kangha**] and then bound up within a turban. Each Sikh is responsible for keeping his own hair washed and clean.

Members of the Khalsa are expected to wear the Five Ks at all times.

All members of the Khalsa keep their hair under control by wearing a kangha.

THE KANGHA

This is the comb which every Sikh should use twice a day. Sikhism places a very great importance on personal hygiene and the long hair must be washed at least every four days. The kangha can also be used to keep the long hair tidy underneath the turban.

Two things are important here:

- The hair is a symbol of that spirituality which is at the heart of Sikhism.
- The comb symbolises the discipline which is needed to keep that spirituality under control.
- Combing the hair with the wooden kangha reminds Sikhs that their lives should be tidy and organised as well.

The kirpan symbolises the spiritual conflict in which all members of the Khalsa are involved.

THE KIRPAN

The **kirpan** [sword] carried by members of the Khalsa can be up to three feet in length. It expresses the power and freedom to be found in Sikhism. It had a practical value at one time but now symbolises the spiritual fight against the powers of evil which every Sikh is called by God to fight. Sikhs in Britain are allowed to carry a kirpan because it is not considered to be an offensive weapon.

We will look at the two remaining Five Ks in Unit 9, together with the spiritual importance of the turban.

OVER TO **YOU** ▶▶▶

1   Sikhs always wear their hair long. What does this symbolise?
2   Sikhs use a kangha to keep their long hair under control. What does this constantly remind the member of the Khalsa of?
3   The sword is an important symbol for all members of the Khalsa. What does it symbolise to Sikhs living in the modern world?

TAKE TIME TO THINK

Why do you think that Guru Gobind Singh placed such a high degree of importance on members of the Khalsa always wearing the Five Ks?

19

THE KARA, THE KACHS AND THE TURBAN

Two of the Five Ks remain:

THE KARA

The **kara** is a steel bangle that is worn on the right wrist. The circle itself is an important Sikh symbol. It forms part of the design on a Sikh flag as well as being worn as a bracelet. It is not just an ornament but serves as a constant reminder that:

The kara – a reminder of the infinity of God.

CHECK IT OUT

God is eternal.

The bond between Sikh and Sikh can never be broken.

The bracelet reminds every sikh that…

God is one.

The bond between God and the believer cannot be broken.

The bond between God and the believer is eternal.

THE IMPORTANCE OF THE FIVE KS

One Sikh writer has written this about the importance of the Five Ks:

A "*Eliminate symbols my Sikhlings and watch the Khalsa crumble. Take off your turban, cut the hair or throw aside the kara, I can tell you truthfully the result would be embarrassing as well as disastrous. These five symbols have held the Sikhs in united brotherhood. They serve to make a Sikh feel and act like a Sikh. They endow him with courage to accomplish feats which would be otherwise impossible for the average man. To make a long story short, the five symbols have an effect on the person wearing them. They are a manifestation of the eternal Guru.*"

Jeanne Cutler. *A brief Introduction to Sikhism*

THE KACHS

These are trousers or shorts that are worn by both men and women. Hindu holy men tended to wear long cloaks and these were impractical for fighting. By wearing shorts, a Sikh shows that he is always ready to take up arms to defend his faith. They symbolise:

- discipline and readiness.
- a modest form of dress which can be taken to indicate a sexual discipline.

THE TURBAN

Although the turban is not one of the Five Ks, most male Sikhs and some female Sikhs wear it. This is a piece of cloth, about five metres in length, which is wound tightly around the head and tucked into place. It was first worn by Guru Gobind Singh as a symbol of the spiritual power of the united Sikh community. His disciples followed his example and this custom continues today.

Young Sikhs wear a small turban called a **patka**. They replace it with a full turban around the age of eleven.

The turban is the most recognisable symbol of Sikhs.

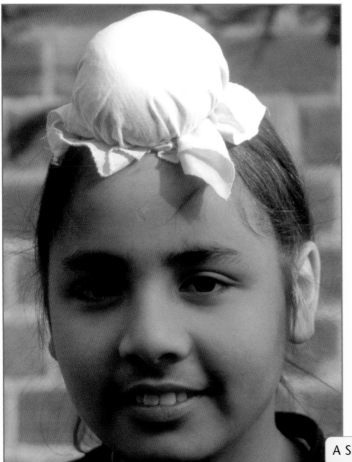

A Sikh child wearing a patka.

OVER TO **YOU** ▶▶▶

Guru Gobind Singh had this to say:

B *"The purpose for which I am born is to spread true religion and to destroy evil doers, root and branch. Blessed are those who keep God in their hearts and a sword in their hands to fight for a noble cause. When there is no other course open to man it is but righteous to unsheathe a sword."*

Dasim Granth

It has been pointed out that Guru Gobind Singh introduced a new military aspect into Sikhism. Which of the Five Ks might have been used for this purpose?

THE GURU GRANTH SAHIB

The Guru Granth Sahib is the last Guru and the most important of all for Sikhs. It is the Word of God. Every day, Sikhs all over the world read their holy book or recite those parts of it that they know by heart. It helps them and guides them in all aspects of their lives.

COMPLETING THE GURU GRANTH SAHIB

In 1706 CE, Guru Gobind Singh added to the Adi Granth hymns that had been written by his father, the ninth Guru. Before he died, Guru Gobind Singh said that the holy book would be the next, and only, Guru. For this reason it was to be called the Guru Granth Sahib.

Since this date, nothing has been added or taken away from the holy book. For many years, copies were written out by hand so that no mistakes were made. The first printed copy was made in 1852.

It was decided that every copy of the Guru Granth Sahib would be exactly the same. This remains true today, with every copy of the holy book:

- having 1430 pages.

- having the different hymns on the same pages.

GUTKAS

Most Sikhs do not have their own copy of the Guru Granth Sahib at home. This is because Sikhs believe that the Guru Granth Sahib is so important that it must have a room of its own at the top of the house – just as any human Guru would be given. The room then becomes a gurdwara because the holy book is installed there.

For the majority of Sikhs this is not practical. Instead, most of them settle for a smaller version called the **gutka**. This contains the most important hymns and prayers. Like the holy book itself, the gutka is treated with the greatest possible respect. It is wrapped in a cloth when it is not being read. Before reading from it, a Sikh washes his or her hands.

THE LANGUAGE OF THE GURU GRANTH SAHIB

Guru Amar Das gathered together the writings of the different Gurus to form the Adi Granth. He used the language of Gurmukhi. This was the language in which Punjabi was written and Punjabi was the language that the people spoke.

This was different to the Hindu holy books. They were written in Sanskrit – a language that was only used for religious worship. When asked why he had not used Sanskrit, Guru Amar Das replied:

A **"***Sanskrit is like a well, deep, inaccessible and confined to the elite. The language of the people is like rainwater, ever fresh, abundant and accessible to all.***"**

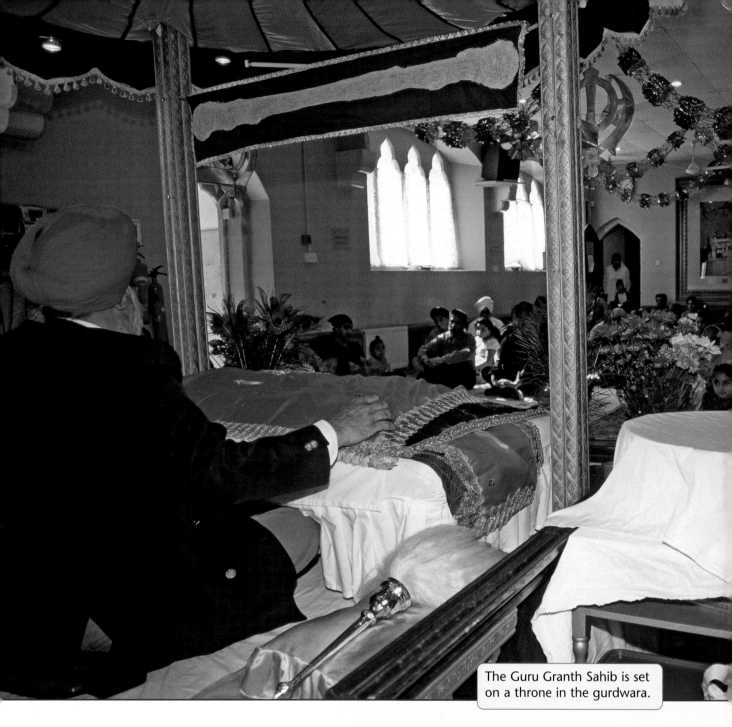

The Guru Granth Sahib is set on a throne in the gurdwara.

OTHER HOLY BOOKS

No other books are as holy as the Guru Granth Sahib. However, Sikhs also read:

- The **Dasam Granth** – the book of the 10th Guru. This contains hymns that were written by Guru Gobind Singh and 52 other poets. Some of these poems are used in Sikh worship.

- The Hukamnamas – letters written by the Gurus to their followers.

- Other books which explain the meaning of different passages in the Guru Granth Sahib.

OVER TO **YOU** ▶▶▶

1 Why were the early copies of the Guru Granth Sahib all made by hand?

2 What is a gutka and why is a Sikh likely to have one?

TAKE TIME TO THINK

Why do you think that Guru Amar Das chose Gurmukhi rather than Sanskrit as the language for the Guru Granth Sahib?

SIKHS AND THE GURU GRANTH SAHIB

You will find out

- Ways in which Sikhs show the respect they have for the Guru Granth Sahib.

- Some of the teachings of the Guru Granth Sahib.

In the glossary

Chauri

Gurdwara

Guru

Guru Granth Sahib

Guru Nanak

Mool Mantra

Romala

The Guru Granth Sahib is never left unattended while it is in the gurdwara.

Sikhs believe that the Guru Granth Sahib is the truth of God – as that truth was revealed to the various Gurus. It is the Word of God. This is why the holy book is treated with the greatest possible respect. Sikh worship can take place only if the Guru Granth Sahib is present – and any building which holds a copy of the holy book automatically becomes a gurdwara.

TREATING THE HOLY BOOK WITH RESPECT

Sikhs show respect for the Guru Granth Sahib in many different ways:

CHECK IT OUT

Showing respect for the Guru Granth Sahib

It sits on a stool and never on the ground.

It rests on a cloth and three cushions, with a canopy over it.

It is always carried above the heads of the worshippers.

Someone always sits behind it.

When the book is closed, it is covered with a special cloth called a **romala**.

This person holds a **chauri**, which is waved over the holy book.

WHAT DOES THE GURU GRANTH SAHIB TEACH?

The Guru Granth Sahib begins with the Mool Mantra. This contains the most basic of all Sikh teachings – those about God:

A "*There is one and only one God Whose Name is truth.*
God the creator is without fear, without hate, immortal,
Without form, and is beyond birth and death,
And is understood through the Guru's grace."

Elsewhere, Guru Nanak describes his own call to preach the truth:

B "*The Ambrosial Nectar of the True Name has become my food. Those who follow the Guru's Teachings, who eat this food and are satisfied, find peace. His minstrel spreads His Glory, singing and vibrating the Word of His Shabad. O Nanak, praising the True Lord, I have obtained His Perfection.*"

Guru Granth Sahib 150

The equality of the sexes is also an important theme. Guru Nanak explained why this is important:

C "*From woman, man is born; within woman, man is conceived; to woman he is engaged and married. Woman becomes his friend; through woman, the future generations come. So why call her bad? From her, kings are born. From woman, woman is born; without woman, there would be no one at all.*"

Guru Granth Sahib 473

OVER TO YOU ▶▶▶

1 Why do Sikhs show the Guru Granth Sahib the greatest possible respect?
2 Write down three things that the Mool Mantra teaches about God – and then add a sentence to explain what you think they mean.
3 What do those who follow Guru Nanak's teachings find?
4 Describe four reasons that Guru Nanak gave for teaching that men and women are equal – and should be treated as such.

TAKE TIME TO THINK

How do you think that worshippers in one other religion you have studied show their respect for their holy book?

For most Sikhs, the only opportunity they have to read from the Guru Granth Sahib is when they are in the gurdwara.

THE GURU GRANTH SAHIB IN THE SIKH COMMUNITY

Sikhs believe that the spirit that was passed down from one Guru to another finally came to rest in the Guru Granth Sahib. It is this spirit that is treated with the greatest respect by all Sikhs. The holy book is treated as if it is a living Guru.

RESPECTING THE HOLY BOOK

As soon as Guru Gobind Singh completed the finished book in 1708, he announced that it would be the next, and last, Guru. It would become the visible symbol of God's presence with the people.

For this reason, it is treated with the greatest possible respect. It is:

- placed, if possible in a room of its own.
- always carried above the heads of the people in the gurdwara.
- placed in an elevated position where everyone can see it.
- opened with a prayer before any act of worship can begin.
- not opened at night. It is 'put to bed' each night with special evening prayers and 'woken up' again in the morning.

THE USE OF THE GURU GRANTH SAHIB

The holy book is used by Sikhs to symbolise the presence of God at very important times in the live of the worshippers:

- when a baby is named.
- when a person is initiated into the Khalsa.
- when two Sikhs are married.
- when a Sikh has died.

Some Sikhs do have individual copies of the Guru Granth Sahib at home but they are mostly found in the gurdwara. If they have their own copy then they must treat it with the same respect as if it was in a gurdwara.

OVER TO YOU ▶▶▶

Answer each of these questions in your own words:

1 The Guru Granth Sahib is located in a gurdwara, sitting on a throne underneath a canopy. What do you think a Sikh is expected to learn from this?
2 What is the link between the Guru Granth Sahib and the Gurus of the past?
3 What part does the Guru Granth Sahib play in the everyday lives of individual Sikhs?

The Guru Granth Sahib is the visible symbol of God's presence.

THE GURDWARA

- About the Sikh place of worship – the gurdwara.
- What happens at the end of each day in a gurdwara.

In the glossary

Ardas

Chauri

Granthi

Gurdwara

Guru

Guru Granth Sahib

Hukam

Khalsa

Khanda

Nishan Sahib

Romala

Takht

You can always recognise a gurdwara by the flag outside.

The word 'gurdwara' means 'the door to the Guru':

- Dwara means 'door' or 'gate'.
- Guru refers to the scriptures.

In other words, the gurdwara is the place where the teachings of the Gurus can be studied, read and meditated on. All of these are important activities for a Sikh. One of the holy books underlines the importance that the gurdwara has for all Sikhs:

A "*Study of and meditation on the scriptures within the congregation is very important, and Sikhs should visit the gurdwara as often as possible.*"

Rahit Maryada

THE GURDWARA

Gurdwaras come in all shapes and sizes but they all have a saffron flag flying outside. On the flag is the symbol of the Khalsa, known as the khanda, which takes its name from the double-edged sword in the centre. The flag is called the **nishan sahib**.

Inside the gurdwara, there is:

- A main worship hall. This is a plain room, although it may have some pictures of the Gurus. These pictures are not worshipped.
- An area where the shoes are left – as these are removed on entering the building. This is a way of showing respect.
- A notice saying that alcohol and tobacco are prohibited in the building. This is another way of showing respect.

The focus of attention in the worship hall is at the front. There is a raised platform, the **takht** or throne, in the centre. It usually has a canopy above it. This can be decorated with streamers and gold or silver tinsel. It is where the Guru Granth Sahib rests, on cushions on a small stool. When it is not being read, it is covered by beautifully embroidered cloths.

The **granthi** often stands behind the holy book, like a soldier on guard, protecting it as he or she waves a chauri. This is a fan made of hair or feathers. This is a symbol of authority and is waved over the Guru Granth Sahib from time to time. In a similar way, it would have been waved over the head of a king or prince in India as a recognition of their importance.

OVER TO **YOU** ▶▶▶

1 Why is the Sikh place of worship called a gurdwara?
2 Imagine that you are paying your first visit to a gurdwara. Write a letter to a friend describing what you saw and what you were expected to do.

AT THE END OF THE DAY

There is always a room in the gurdwara where the Guru Granth Sahib is laid to rest at night. This is a private room high in the gurdwara. It contains a bed which is covered with romalas.

At the end of the day, everyone stands as the granthi faces the holy book and says the Ardas prayer, before making a hukam. The Guru Granth Sahib is carefully wrapped in a clean cloth. The head of the granthi is also covered by a cloth. The Guru Granth Sahib is placed on his head and another person stands in front, waving the chauri. The holy book is then taken to its resting place for the night. It will be returned in the same way early next morning.

TAKE TIME TO THINK

Why do you think that Sikhism stresses the importance of studying and meditating on the scriptures 'within the congregation'?

Everyone entering a gurdwara must leave their shoes outside as a mark of respect to God.

29

THE LANGAR

You will find out

- The example set by Guru Nanak in eating with everyone who travelled to see him.

- The lessons that Sikhs learn from eating together.

- The important role that the langar plays in the religious life of Sikhs.

In the glossary

Gurdwara

Guru Nanak

Langar

THE EXAMPLE OF GURU NANAK

It was Guru Amar Das who established the tradition of building a langar, a communal dining room, attached to every gurdwara. In doing this, he was following the example of Guru Nanak, who encouraged people to eat together when they travelled to see him. In fact, he told them that they should enjoy a meal together before they brought their worries and problems to him.

Guru Nanak did this for three reasons:

- To feed those who were hungry and poor, plus those who had travelled a long way to see him and were weary after their journey.

- To teach people that everyone was equal in the sight of God and eating together was an effective way of expressing this.

- To oppose the old Hindu Caste System, which taught that people were not equal – a system that Guru Nanak totally rejected.

As a result, every Sikh act of worship concluded with a meal and this still happens today.

IN THE LANGAR

The langar is an 'open kitchen' and there is one attached to every gurdwara. While a service is going on, some Sikhs are busy working in the kitchen preparing a meal for the people to eat at the end of the service. Both men and women work together in the langar and the service is often relayed to them over loudspeakers.

If someone in the gurdwara is celebrating a special anniversary, then they often provide the ingredients for the meal as a way of celebrating the event. The meal is always vegetarian. There is a good reason for this. Everyone in the congregation is expected to stay and join in the meal. If it is vegetarian, it means that no one can be offended by what they eat.

As soon as the service is over, everyone moves into the langar to eat the meal. Those who have prepared the meal and those who serve it do so as an act of service, a sewa, to God and the community. Sikhs and non-Sikhs are invited to participate. This is to follow the teaching of Guru Arjan Dev, who said:

A   "*Let all share equally, no one should be seen as an outsider.*"

TAKE TIME TO THINK

Equality means that people have the same rights and are treated with the same respect as everyone else.

a) Do you think that everyone is treated fairly and equally in our society?

b) Can you think of any reasons and examples where people are treated differently?

Both men and women work alongside each other in the langar to show true sexual equality.

OVER TO **YOU** ▶▶▶

1 When they are eating in the langar, everyone sits to eat at the same level – usually on the floor. What lesson do you think that Sikhs are expected to learn from this?

2 More than one religion treats meals as very important – and a spiritual occasion. Describe another occasion on which this happens. Explain why you think that meals have this significance.

Waiting on tables in the langar is a true act of sewa.

SIKH WORSHIP

You will find out

- About services held in a gurdwara.

- Why these services are important to Sikhs.

- About karah parshad and its importance to Sikhs.

In the glossary

Gurdwara

Guru

Guru Granth Sahib

Guru Nanak

Hukam

Karah Parshad

Kirpan

Sikhs do not keep any special holy day during the week. Worshippers come together on the most convenient day of the week. In Britain, this is usually a Sunday, although many Sikhs visit the gurdwara to pray in front of the Guru Granth Sahib at other times during the week.

A SERVICE IN THE GURDWARA

Before visiting a gurdwara to pray, a Sikh must bathe. On entering the gurdwara, he or she touches the flagpole, the step and then, with the same hand, their forehead. This is in accordance with the words in the Guru Granth Sahib:

A *"Wherever my Sat Guru goes and sits, that place is beautiful, O Lord King. The Guru's disciples seek that place and take and apply its dust to their foreheads."*

A service in a gurdwara lasts for several hours. People may come and go as they please, although everyone is expected to be there at the close.

An important part is reached in the service when the Guru Granth Sahib is opened at random and a reading given, starting at the top left-hand corner of the page. This reading is called a hukam [the will of God]. Sikhs believe that God speaks to them through this reading.

Hymn-singing is an important part of every service and is led by a group of musicians. They sing hymns from the Guru Granth Sahib – many of which are believed to have been written by Guru Nanak himself.

Services in a gurdwara go on for a long time – with people able to come and go.

Musicians in a gurdwara play a very important role in the services.

WHY ARE SERVICES IMPORTANT?

There are three important reasons why Sikhs hold religious services:

- It provides an opportunity for every worshipper to reflect and meditate on the words of the Guru Granth Sahib – the words of God. Although Sikhs can have a copy of the holy book at home, most of them do not. Coming to the gurdwara provides the only opportunity that the majority have to study it.
- It gives individual Sikhs the experience of worshipping together and especially of joining with other Sikhs in singing hymns.
- It provides a practical expression of that unity and equality which is so highly valued within the Sikh community.

KARAH PARSHAD

Every service in a gurdwara draws to a close with the eating of karah parshad – holy food. This food is prepared before the service begins and then a kirpan is used to give it a final stir as the service closes. The sweetness of the holy food is a reminder to everyone of the goodness of God. Its sharing with all, including non-Sikhs, shows that no one is allowed to leave God's house spiritually hungry. These words are said as a service draws to a close in a gurdwara:

B "*Our right and wrong deeds will be judged at Your court. Some will be seated near Your seat; some will be kept at a distance for ever. The work has ended for those who have worshipped You. O Nanak, their faces are lit with joy, and they set free many others.*"

OVER TO YOU ▶▶▶

1   What are three things that a Sikh does before entering a gurdwara for a service?
2   What is a hukam and why is it important?
3   What are the three reasons why Sikhs attend public worship in a gurdwara?

TAKE TIME TO THINK

Reflection and meditation is an important part of the Sikh religious experience. Do you ever reflect and meditate? If so, on what?

PRAYER AND MEDITATION

You will find out

- The important part that prayer plays in the everyday life of a Sikh.

- The Ardas prayer.

In the glossary

Ardas

Gurdwara

Guru

Japji

Khalsa

Rahiras

Waheguru

Prayer forms a very important part of the life of every Sikh believer.

Prayer is a very important part of religious faith in Sikhism. A prayer is said, for example, before every meal. Sikhs who belong to the Khalsa also promise to say certain prayers each day, though every Sikh tries to set time aside during the day to pray and think about God.

PRAYER IN THE HOME

Sikhs living outside India may find it difficult to make time to pray regularly – especially in the morning. They try, therefore, to pray while they are doing something else like preparing the breakfast or travelling to work.

Sikhs vary in the way that they say their prayers:

CHECK IT OUT

say the whole of the morning prayer – the Japji.

say the first five verses of the Japji.

end the day by reciting the **Rahiras**, thanking God for all the successes of the day.

In their prayers, some Sikhs…

simply recite the word 'Waheguru', meaning 'Wonderful Lord'.

remind themselves that there is one all-powerful God.

The Rahiras addresses God as "You the giver. You the Receiver".

PRAYER IN THE GURDWARA

As we saw in Unit 15, Sikhs meet together regularly in the gurdwara to pray and worship. The Ardas prayer is the most important part of the service and all of the people stand to say it together. This prayer asks everyone present to remember God and the Gurus and to think of those who have died for the Sikh faith.

It also asks God to keep all Sikhs faithful to Him and to bless the whole world. At the end of the prayer, the words "Waheguru ji khalsa, Waheguru ji ki fateh" are said. This means "The Khalsa belongs to God, victory belongs to God". The same words are also said on other special occasions, such as weddings.

Extracts A and B are taken from two Sikh prayers:

A *"Forgetting God even for an instant is a great affliction of the mind."*

B *"Call upon God with every breath, who has made you high in the range of creation. This invaluable stage of existence is attained through grace. You must offer all your love."*

OVER TO YOU ▶▶▶

1 How might Sikhs find time to pray if they lead a very busy life?

2 What do Sikhs try to remind themselves of about God at the start of every day?

3 What kind of successes do you think you might remember at the end of a day if you were a Sikh?

TAKE TIME TO THINK

Sikhs are encouraged to think of God every moment of the day but do you think this is really possible – and, if so, how?

It is mainly the responsibility of a Sikh father to teach his children how to pray.

THE HARIMANDIR

Sikhs believe that every gurdwara is equally important because each one holds a copy of the Guru Granth Sahib. However, the Harimadir Sahib at Amritsar holds a unique place in the affections of the Sikh community.

Harimandir Sahib means 'the temple of God'. It was begun when Guru Amar Das, the third Guru, asked Ram Das (later the 4th Guru) to build a place that would be the central meeting place for all Sikhs. Work began excavating the lake in 1577 and it was finally completed by the 5th Guru in 1588. Work then began on the temple, which was completed in 1601.

CHECK IT OUT

The Harimandir…

- stands in the middle of a lake, called the Pool of Nectar, which is reached by a causeway 60 metres long.
- is 12 metres square, surrounded by a marble walkway.
- has four entrances, one on each side, to show it is open to people coming from the four corners of the Earth.

THE GOLDEN TEMPLE

The Harimandir has been damaged several times. In 1764 it was rebuilt in marble and the upper part of the building was covered in copper sheets, overlaid with gold. Since this happened, it has been known as the Golden Temple.

The walkway which surrounds the lake is known as the parkama and this is made from marble. Each side is about 150 metres long. There are shrines and memorials to different Sikh leaders who have been killed defending their faith. As Sikhs walk around it in a clockwise direction, so they scatter rose petals or lay garlands at the shrines.

The causeway across which pilgrims pass on their way to the Golden Temple.

The Golden Temple is at the very heart of the religion of Sikhism.

CARRYING THE GURU GRANTH SAHIB

Continual readings from the Guru Granth Sahib begin at dawn in the Golden Temple and go on till late at night. At five o'clock each morning and at ten o'clock each night, the holy book is carried to and from the worship room where it spends the night.

The Guru Granth Sahib is carried, resting on cushions, by the head granthi. It is a great honour for a Sikh to take part in this procession and it may take a long time to complete – because many Sikhs want to participate. As the Guru Granth Sahib is read during the day so thousands of worshippers pass through the Temple.

GURU NANAK AND PILGRIMAGES

Thousands of pilgrims visit the Golden Temple each day, although Guru Nanak warned his followers against making a holy pilgrimage:

A "*If a man goes to bathe at a place of pilgrimage, and he has the mind of a crook and the body of a thief, of course his outside will be washed by the bathing, but his inside will be twice as unclean. He will be like a gourd which is clean on the outside but full of poison on the inside. The saints are pure without such bathing. The thief remains a thief even if he bathes at places of pilgrimage.*"

Guru Granth Sahib 789

OVER TO YOU ▶▶▶

1 What does the word 'Harimandir' mean?
2 What great change to the Harimandir took place in 1764?
3 Imagine that you make your first visit to the Golden Temple in Amritsar. Describe what you see around you in an e-mail to your parents.

You can obtain some more information from: www.sikhnet.com/GoldenTemple

TAKE TIME TO THINK

Many Sikhs wanted the Harimandir to be as high and as splendid as possible. Instead it was given the lowest possible elevation. Why do you think this was?

37

FAMILY LIFE

The family is the key to Sikh relationships and to the outlook of every Sikh on life. It is in the family that Sikhs:

- first become aware of God.

- learn how to live with other people.

- gain the right values to see them through life.

- learn how to pray.

The Sikh Gurus often asked the question:

A *"Why look for God in the forest when God is at home?"*

Guru Granth Sahib 684

They were attacking the Hindu practice of men spending time in forests and desert places, denying themselves all earthly pleasure in search of God. As Guru Nanak taught:

B *"Practising self-torture to subdue desires only wears out the body. The mind is not subdued through fasting and penances."*

Guru Granth Sahib 905

Sikhs do not believe in practising celibacy.

In a Sikh family, young people are expected to show great respect for their elders.

THE MARRIED LIFE IS THE RIGHT LIFE

Sikhism teaches that every man should marry, if possible. Only one Guru was unmarried – and he died at the age of eight! The 4th Guru, Ram Das, composed the wedding hymn, the **Lavan**, showing that marriage is part of God's plan for everyone. This is why Sikh marriages always take place in the presence of the Guru Granth Sahib. This guarantees that God will bless the relationship.

It is usual to have a head of the extended family. In Sikh families this can be either male or female. If it is a man then someone will tie his turban in public to show that he has been chosen. In the case of a woman, however, there is no public ceremony.

This family offers great support for its members. If any child loses its parents, for example, it will be adopted by relatives. If aged parents are unable to look after themselves then one of their sons will care for them – usually the youngest. He is likely to have the fewest responsibilities and still be in need of guidance from his parents.

THE FAMILY DECIDES

Extended families often choose marriage partners for their children because it is a matter of great concern to a family when a new person joins it. They may not fit in. Families also choose the careers of their children. Children often work with members of their own family and they need someone who can supply a necessary skill.

Some idea of the importance of family life in the Sikh community can be seen from the way that close friends are often called 'sister' or 'brother'. To be made an honorary family member is a mark of great respect.

OVER TO **YOU** ▶▶▶

1 Guru Nanak warned that domestic involvement is a whirlpool. What do you think he had in mind when he said this?

2 Give some reasons for the Sikh belief that the family is the unit that God most approves of.

3 What do you think you would bear in mind if you were the head of a Sikh family, looking for a husband for your daughter who is a teacher and a wife for your son who is a farmer?

TAKE TIME TO THINK

If your son or daughter questioned you about your desire to be involved in the choice of their wife or husband, what reasons would you give them?

THE NAME-GIVING CEREMONY

The birth of any child, boy or girl, is welcomed in a Sikh family as a gift from God. He or she begins to learn about their Sikh faith from the moment they are born. As soon as possible after birth, the father whispers the Mool Mantra [A] into the baby's ear before a drop of honey is placed on his or her lips. The Mool Mantra is the most important statement of Sikh belief.

A *"There is but one God whose name is True, the Creator, devoid of fear and enmity, immortal, unborn, self-existent, great and bountiful. The True One was in the beginning, the True One was in the primal age. The True One is, was, O Nanak, and the True One also shall be."*

THE CEREMONY

As soon as the mother is well enough, after giving birth, the whole family goes to the gurdwara:

- The parents take with them the ingredients for making karah parshad and a small, embroidered romala.

- Amrit is made by dissolving sugar crystals in water and the solution – called 'the nectar of life' – is stirred by the granthi with a khanda.

- The granthi places the khanda in the amrit and then puts some on the baby's lips.

- The granthi opens the Guru Granth Sahib at random. The first word on the left-hand page is then read to the parents. They choose a name for the baby beginning with the first letter of the first word. The granthi announces the baby's name to the congregation.

The ceremony is now almost over. All that remains is a final reading and the sharing of karah parshad with the whole congregation. Presents are exchanged and most people make a donation to help poor widows and other deserving causes in the community. Sometimes the parents also arrange for the Guru Granth Sahib to be read through from beginning to end without a break. This is known as the **Akhand Path.** It can also be done on other important occasions.

WHY IS NAME-GIVING SO IMPORTANT?

There are three reasons why this particular ceremony is such an important part of Sikh worship:

- It is a public announcement by the parents that they accept their child as a gift from God.

- It provides an opportunity for the mother and father to thank God for the safe delivery of their baby.

- It provides the baby with a name which will carry a great deal of personal and religious significance throughout its life.

A Sikh baby is being baptised and dedicated to God.

TAKE TIME TO THINK

This prayer is one that can be used in the name-giving ceremony:

B "*I present this child, and with thy grace, I administer to him [her] amrit. May he [she] be a true Sikh. May he [she] devote himself [herself] to the service of his [her] fellows and motherland.*"

What do you think "a true Sikh" is?

OVER TO YOU ▶▶▶

1 A baby has just been born into a Sikh family of a friend of yours and you have been invited along to the name-giving ceremony. Describe what happens in the ceremony.

2 Explain why the name-giving ceremony is very important for all Sikhs.

3 Look at the prayer from the name-giving ceremony in Extract B. What does this prayer hope that the child will grow up to be?

SERVING OTHERS

You will find out

- The important place that service has for every Sikh.

- What serving others involves.

- The meaning of daswandh.

In the glossary

Gurdwara

Gurmukhi

Guru Granth Sahib

Guru Nanak

Japji

Langar

Nit-Nem

Rahiras

In a Sikh home, prayers are said in the morning, evening and last thing at night. These are set prayers known as **Nit-Nem**, the 'daily rule'. Sikhs learn the Gurmukhi language so that they can say these prayers and read the scriptures.

> *"Our daily prayers are intended to make us more like Guru Nanak as we read about him in the Guru Granth Sahib. This is also why we say other prayers, such as the Japji and the Rahiras, during the day. Although we are really praying for others, we are also praying that our own sins will be forgiven. We ask God that everything will be good for everyone and we try to do this every day."*

Mahendra, 15

Sikhs learn about their faith at home and in the gurdwara. They also find out about other religions because they are expected to help people of all religions and cultures. They believe that all people are brothers and sisters who have been created by God.

SERVING OTHERS

Serving others is the highest ideal for every Sikh to follow in their daily life. There are three different kinds of service:

- Manual labour – physical work. This might be needed if someone is ill, disabled or elderly. It might include preparing and serving food in the langar – the free kitchen attached to every gurdwara. It is particularly important that those who are rich, clever or important should work alongside others to provide this kind of service. This benefits everyone and everyone learns from it.

- Intellectual service – using your mind to help others. This might include, for example, serving on the committee that is responsible for running the gurdwara.

- Material help – the most common kind of service that everyone can provide. Everyone, for example, can pass on clothes that they no longer use to families in need or to charity shops.

Guru Nanak taught that placing oneself at the service of others is the most important thing that a person can do. He commented that, if someone wanted to take a seat in the court of God [heaven], then they should dedicate themselves, in this life, to serving others.

TAKE TIME TO THINK

Even if you are not a Sikh, do you think that it is important to serve others? If so, in what ways do you think this can be done?

DASWANDH

To help Sikhs appreciate the importance of sacrifice and sharing, they should give 1/10 of their wealth [daswandh] to those in need. This money can then be used in different ways:

CHECK IT OUT

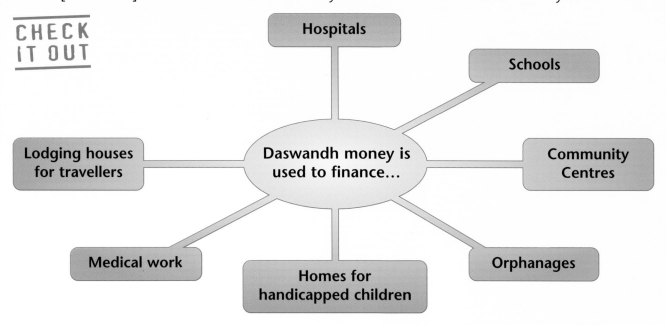

Hospitals

Schools

Lodging houses for travellers

Daswandh money is used to finance...

Community Centres

Medical work

Homes for handicapped children

Orphanages

Working in the langar and preparing food for others is a very common way of service open to all Sikhs.

OVER TO **YOU** ▶▶▶

1 The Guru Granth Sahib warns that a person who has too much money is burdened with care while the person who has too little is always trying to find more. Only the person who has neither too much nor too little is at peace with himself.

 a) Do you agree with this comment?

 b) What do you think are some of the dangers of having too much money?

 c) Do you think it is the person who has just enough who finds peace?

2 The Sikh who wants to find entrance to the Courts of God is advised to serve others. In what different ways is a Sikh told to do this?

MARRIAGE AND DIVORCE

In the Sikh community, marriage is not simply an arrangement between two people. It is the intertwining of two families. For this reason, the two families have to be acceptable to each other and this is why they are involved in the choice of their son's or daughter's marriage partner. Three conditions have to be met for a marriage to take place:

- The couple must both be Sikh believers.
- The couple must have been introduced and be willing to accept each other as partners for life.
- The bride and groom must give their full and free assent to marriage.

ANAND KARAJ [THE CEREMONY OF BLISS]

The Sikh wedding ceremony is called the **Anand Karaj** – the Ceremony of Bliss. Wedding ceremonies in Britain are conducted in a gurdwara because the Guru Granth Sahib must be present to make it valid.

In the service:

- The morning hymn is sung, explaining how the couple can find happiness together.
- The bride and groom show that they are entering into marriage freely by bowing in front of the Guru Granth Sahib.
- Garlands are placed around the necks of the couple and on the Guru Granth Sahib by the bride's father, who takes the groom's saffron scarf, passes it over his shoulder and places the end in the bride's hand. The couple are now joined together.
- The wedding hymn – the Lavan – is sung, which speaks of the love of God and the union of the self or spirit with God.
- The couple then walk four times around the Guru Granth Sahib [see below] in a clockwise direction. As they walk, flower petals are thrown over them to symbolise the fragrance of their new life together.
- The service ends, as all services in a gurdwara, with the Ardas prayer; a random reading from the Guru Granth Sahib and the sharing of karah parshad.

CHECK IT OUT

The four circlings indicate:

STEP ONE shows that marriage is God's will for everyone.

STEP TWO stirs the first feelings of love as the bride leaves her old life behind to build a new life with her husband.

STEP THREE symbolises the bride's feelings of detachment from the world and her new attachment to her husband.

STEP FOUR is a reminder of the perfect love that can exist between two people.

During the wedding ceremony, the couple walk four times around the Guru Granth Sahib in a clockwise direction.

DIVORCE

Divorce is very rare among traditional Sikh families, although it is increasingly common among those living in Western countries. If a marriage cannot be saved then divorce is allowed. This permits the man and the woman to remarry in a gurdwara.

A *"They are not husband and wife who have physical contact only. Only they are truly married who have one spirit in two bodies."*

Sikh hymn

OVER TO **YOU** ▶▶▶

1 What are the conditions that need to be met before a Sikh marriage can go ahead?

2 Four circuits of the Guru Granth Sahib take place during the wedding ceremony. What is the meaning and significance of each of these journeys?

TAKE TIME TO THINK

Look at the quotation from the Sikh hymn in Extract A. Explain, in your own words, what you think it means.

A SIKH FUNERAL

Facing death, a Sikh is comforted by readings from the scriptures. A favourite passage, often read in the last hours of a person's life, is Guru Arjan Dev's Hymn of Peace [A]:

A *"With your eyes behold the splendour of God's presence. The company of the faithful will banish every other presence from your sight. Walk in the way of God. With every step you take you will be treading down evil inclinations. With your hands do God's work and with your eyes listen to his instructions. Thus your life will be rounded off with God's approval which will be reflected in your face."*

It was Guru Nanak who said:

B *"The dawn of a new day is the message of a sunset."*

CREMATION

Sikhs feel great sadness at the loss of a loved one. Yet it is hope rather than sadness that should mark the death of every Sikh. Death removes the last barrier that exists between the person and his or her God.

The cremation service is deliberately kept very simple. The first act after death is for relatives to wash the body and then, if the person was a member of the Khalsa, to dress it in the Five Ks.

The body is then taken in procession to the place of cremation. The mourners sing hymns and the cortege is often followed by a band. As the funeral pyre on which the body has been placed is lit by the elder son, so the evening hymn, the Sohilla [C], is sung. This hymn expresses just how Sikhs feel, and what they believe, about life after death:

- Every person possesses a part of God which will, eventually, return to God.

- This part of God, the soul, can never die.

- It is a combination of good works and religious acts of devotion that make it possible for the soul to return to God.

C *"Know the real purpose of being here and gather up the treasure under the guidance of the Guru. Make your mind God's home. If he abides with you undisturbed you will not be reborn... Strive to seek that for which you have come into the world and through the grace of the Guru, God will dwell in your heart."*

A TIME OF MOURNING

Sikhs set aside a specific time for mourning the loss of a loved one. There are two ways of doing this:

- A continual reading [Akhand Path] of the whole Guru Granth Sahib, which may take place in the 48 hours following death.

- A 7 day reading or a 10 day reading of the Guru Granth Sahib in the home of the dead person. Close relatives say special prayers for the dead person for 10 days in either the gurdwara or at home.

Sikhs are not allowed to erect memorials or gravestones.

OVER TO **YOU** ▶▶▶

1 Read Guru Arjan's Hymn of Peace in Extract A. What does this have to say about how a Sikh should live now?

2 What does the Hymn of Peace have to say about how a Sikh should face death and what encouragement does it offer?

TAKE TIME TO THINK

Why do you think that Sikhs are not allowed to erect memorials or gravestones to a dead relative? What do you think is the reason behind it?

At a Sikh funeral, the coffin is left open so that people can pay their last respects.

SIKHS AND LIFE AFTER DEATH

You will find out

- The Sikh belief in reincarnation.
- Human inequality and how Sikhs explain it.
- The illustration of the snake and its skin.

In the glossary

Guru Nanak

Reincarnation

Sikhs believe that the soul of this man has lived many times before.

While Guru Nanak was very sympathetic to many of the teachings of Islam, he could not accept its view of life after death. Instead, he followed the teaching of Hinduism that many lives on Earth are necessary before a person is fit for the afterlife. This belief is called **reincarnation**.

REINCARNATION

It is the teaching of Sikhism that a person's soul is a minute part of the Eternal Soul or God. The soul has existed since the time of creation. It is now waiting to be reabsorbed back into the Eternal Soul. In the meantime, it lives in a whole succession of different bodies.

The human soul has evolved from the most primitive forms of life before reaching its present state – the highest possible state of existence. This is the point from which it hopes to reach reunion with God. As Guru Arjan Dev said:

A *"Since you have now acquired this human frame, this is your opportunity to become one with God; All other labours are of no use; Seek the company of the holy and glorify God's Name."*

OVER TO YOU ▶▶▶

1 This verse is read at Sikh funerals:

   B *"Why believe that the mortal body is permanent? It passes away like a dream in the night, like the shadow of the clouds. Those who realise that the world is unreal seek protection in God."*

   What do you think about the human body? Is it all that we have or is there more to human beings?

2 Apart from the Sikh scriptures and other religious writings, can you think of any facts of experience that might lead someone to believe in reincarnation?

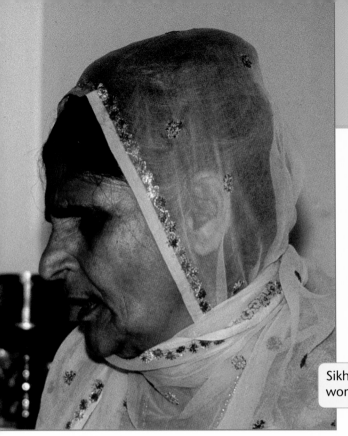

Sikhs hope that this might be the last time that this woman lives before being reabsorbed back into God.

HUMAN INEQUALITY

Guru Nanak was very concerned about the poor and the outcasts. He believed that God is available to everyone – beggars and rulers, rich and poor, men and women. The inequality to be found in all life is brought about by human behaviour – both in this life and in past lives.

A person's lot in life is of their own making. If someone is born into poor circumstances, they have to improve their own situation – Guru Nanak attacked the idlers and parasites who waited for others to help them.

Although people make their own fate and future, it is always the will of God that is being worked out:

C "*By His writ some have pleasure, others pain,*
By His grace some are saved,
Others doomed to die, relive and die again;
His will encompasseth all, there is none beside,
O Nanak, who knows, hath no ego and hath no pride."
Japji prayer

THE SNAKE AND ITS SKIN

To the Sikh, heaven and hell are not future places of judgement. If they exist then they are here and now. Birth and death are changes in the course of a person's life. As a snake casts off its old skin, so the soul leaves the body at death and takes on a new one. Fortunately, the soul leaves behind its old guilt and so has the chance of moving a little closer to the Eternal Spirit.

TAKE TIME TO THINK

In what ways do you think a belief in reincarnation might affect:

a) The way that a person lives in this life?
b) The way that a person thinks about their own death?
c) The way that members of the Sikh community live?

49

SIKHISM AND A FAIRER WORLD

You will find out

- The responsibility that Sikhs feel to give to the poor.
- The two forms in which help is given to the poor in the world.
- The work carried out by Khalsa Aid.

In the glossary

Gurdwara

Guru

Guru Nanak

Langar

Nam

In every gurdwara service, worshippers give money to help the poor. This is a spiritual offering made to God.

Sikhism does not teach that there is any spiritual value in being poor. As Extract A shows, poverty and a lack of money can only lead to great anxiety for those who are affected. For this reason, Sikhs must do everything they can to relieve the poverty of others through selfless service and giving money.

A *"Those without money have the anxiety of poverty."*

Guru Granth Sahib 1019

THE RESPONSIBILITY TO GIVE

Sikhs believe that God, **Nam**, has been generous in all the gifts he has given the world. Many, though, have been given more than they need to meet their own requirements and the needs of those who depend on them. They must do all they can to relieve poverty throughout the world.

The sharing of wealth will lead to the gradual building up of a fairer world. This is the spiritual objective of every Sikh. It can take place in two different ways:

- **Giving money in the form of aid.** Many Sikhs channel their gifts through Khalsa Aid [see below]. Like other charities, Khalsa Aid provides two kinds of help for those in need:

  1. **Short-term aid.** A quick response to help after there has been a natural disaster such as a flood, a hurricane or an earthquake. These natural disasters are more likely to hit poor than rich countries. A very speedy response is needed when they do. Khalsa Aid works with other charities to provide this help.

  2. **Long-term aid.** This is help needed over many years to build up a poor country's schools, hospitals, drainage and agriculture. Skilled help is needed so that people can learn to help themselves.

- **Food that is donated for use in the langar** – the free kichen attached to every gurdwara.

Sikhs believe that it is against the justice of God that many people should be living in great poverty when there are enough resources to meet everyone's need.

KHALSA AID

Established in 1999, Khalsa Aid is a British based relief organisation founded on two Sikh principles:

- Selfless service
- Universal love

It works to help people in some of the poorest countries in the world – Turkey, Gujarat [West India], the Democratic Republic of the Congo and Somalia. All of the people working for Khalsa Aid are unpaid and are inspired by the teachings of Guru Nanak and the different Sikh Gurus.

OVER TO **YOU** ▶▶▶

1 Why are Sikh believers sure that they must do everything possible to help the poor?

2 'It is not my fault that there are so many poor people in the world. I can do nothing about it.' What do you think a Sikh might say to someone who expressed this opinion?

TAKE TIME TO THINK

Charities working among poor people stress the importance of involving and training local people – and educating people at home. Why do you think these two aspects are thought to be very important?

SIKHISM AND PREJUDICE

You will find out

- Why Sikhs believe that all forms of prejudice are wrong.

- The inheritance that Sikhs have taken over from Hinduism – positive and negative.

In the glossary

Gurdwara

Guru

Guru Gobind Singh

Guru Granth Sahib

Khalsa

Langar

Sikhs believe that the one God is the source of all life. That is a basic Sikh teaching. God has no colour or human form. Differences between male and female, black or white, do not apply to God. Neither should they apply to human beings.

SIKHISM AND PREJUDICE

Sikhs believe that all forms of prejudice – whether based on a person's religion, colour, sex or class – are based on a misunderstanding of the human race. The Sikh Gurus stressed not only the oneness of God but also the oneness of the human race. You can read what Guru Gobind Singh had to say about this in Extract A:

A *"Though they use different dresses according to the influence of regional customs, all men have the same eyes, ears, body and figure made out of the compounds of earth, air, fire and water."*

Guru Gobind Singh

Sikhs believe this despite the fact that God is understood differently by the different religions and society is divided by differences of culture and wealth.

SIKHISM, HINDUISM AND PREJUDICE

Sikhism grew out of Hinduism and this has had two key influences – one positive and the other negative.

THE POSITIVE INFLUENCE

Hinduism is a religion famed for its tolerance of other religions.

- The effect of this on Sikhism is seen in the Guru Granth Sahib, which contains the writings of six of the Gurus – and also from many Muslims and Hindus.

- The Gurus never claimed that the only truth about God was found in Sikhism.

> Guru Gobind Singh, the last of the Sikh Gurus, taught his followers that everyone is equal in the presence of God.

THE NEGATIVE INFLUENCE

Sikhism grew up as a separate religion from Hinduism because of that faith's teaching about the Caste System. This prejudice against lower members of society has no place in the teaching of the Sikh Gurus.

- In Sikh worship, members of all castes must sit together in the gurdwara and eat together in the langar.

- The hymns of two men from lower castes, Kabir and Ravidas [B], are included in the Guru Granth Sahib.

- Ever since Guru Gobind Singh baptised the first Khalsa Sikhs in 1699, Sikhs are given the names Singh [lion] and Kaur [princess] when they enter the brotherhood. Unlike the Hindu family names, which often indicate a person's place in society, these two titles suggest that all people are equal.

B *"Ravidas, the cobbler, praised his Lord for a brief time and from a low caste wretch was purified and all four castes fell at his feet."*

Guru Granth Sahib 733

OVER TO **YOU** ▶▶▶

1 Look at Extract A and explain how the Sikh holy book underlines its teaching that all people are the same – and equal.

2 What is one positive effect and one negative effect that the Hindu religion had upon early Sikhs?

3 How has the Guru Granth Sahib stressed that there is no place for prejudice in Sikhism?

TAKE TIME TO THINK

Do you find traces of prejudice among your friends? If so, what kind of things are they prejudiced about? Can you work out why?

SIKHISM AND THE NATURAL WORLD

You will find out

- The Sikh belief that God created the universe.

- The craziness of human beings harming the planet.

- The balance in nature that human beings must maintain.

- The desire of many Sikhs to follow a vegetarian lifestyle.

In the glossary

Guru

Guru Granth Sahib

Guru Nanak

Langar

Punjab

The Punjab is an agricultural country and, of its many farmers, most are Sikhs. Their concern to improve the yields of their crops in this very poor land has led them to welcome the use of modern technology and chemical fertilisers. The long–term effect of these is only just being felt. The soil is being damaged and rivers are being polluted as surplus water drains back into them.

A disaster took place in Bhopal in 1984. A dense cloud of lethal gas from a chemical factory engulfed the town, killing hundreds of people and scarring thousands for life. People are still being affected by the disaster today – many years later.

Sikhs believe that the whole Earth, with its beauty, is the handiwork of God and so should be cherished.

SIKH TEACHING ON CARING FOR THE PLANET

The Gurus taught that the world belongs to God. One of the names given to God is the Creator, although Sikhs do not bother with any attempt to explain how the world was created. They simply believe that:

A *"The universe comes into being by God's will."*

Guru Granth Sahib 1

Notice the word 'comes' is used instead of 'came'. Sikhs believe that creation is a continuous process. It is still happening.

Sikhs believe that God is within creation. Guru Nanak said:

B *"I see the Creator pervading everywhere."*

Adi Granth 21

If human beings harm creation then they are actually hurting God. This is crazy. Human beings depend on God for all the blessings of the natural world. The arrival of the monsoon waters in the Punjab every year, for example, is literally a matter of life and death. Such is the relief of the people when they do arrive that every Sikh expresses their praise and thankfulness to God.

God created a balance in nature and it is essential that this balance is maintained. These words from Guru Nanak make it clear what principles need to be kept in mind as human beings try to do this:

C *"Pray to God – remember God and God's authority always. Earn an honest living – do not take what does not belong to you or more than you need – essential truths for a proper relationship with nature. Share with others – this includes all creation, not just human beings."*

Guru Nanak pointed out that everything, and everyone, is caught up in the web or chain of life. This has suggested to many Sikhs that they should become vegetarians. Certainly every meal served in the langar is vegetarian – to allow everyone to eat without any offence to anyone.

Yet there are stories of the later Gurus eating meat and even hunting. Out of respect to Hindus, however, beef is always avoided as the cow is a sacred animal in the Hindu religion.

OVER TO YOU ▶▶▶

1 According to Sikh believers, what was the intention of God when he created the Earth?

2 Read Extract C through carefully. What does this quotation say about the relationship between God and nature?

TAKE TIME TO THINK

The Guru Granth Sahib says that the Gurus have made us aware of our responsibilities to the Earth. What do you think are the most important of those responsibilities?

THE ROLE OF WOMEN IN SIKHISM

When Guru Nanak founded Sikhism, there were many Hindu beliefs about women that he wanted to disown. Here are three of them:

- That women are ritually unclean when they menstruate and give birth.

- That a girl in a family is a liability whose marriage simply drains the family's resources. This led to the killing of baby girls soon after birth – a common practice at the time known as **infanticide**.

- That widows are the bearers of bad luck. This led to a ban on widows remarrying.

He reserved his greatest condemnation, however, for the Hindu custom of encouraging wives to throw themselves on the burning funeral pyres of their husbands – a practice called **sati**. Both this and infanticide continued in many Sikh communities until the end of the 19th century.

THE TEACHING OF THE GURUS

To raise the status of women, the Sikh Gurus established **grihasth** – the life of the householder or married person – as the ideal and normal way of life for most Sikhs. This changed the Sikh attitude towards women in three ways:

- It became accepted that both men and women could reach union with God by constantly remembering God and carrying out their household duties at the same time. Wherever they are and whatever they are doing, they can constantly repeat the name of God under their breath.

- A woman does not need to wait for rebirth as a man before she can reach **moksha**. She can reach it as a woman.

- Sexual faithfulness to one's partner is as important for a man as it is for a woman.

This extract from the Guru Granth Sahib underlines the very important part that women play as wives and mothers:

A *"It is through woman, the despised one, that we are conceived and from her that we are born. It is to woman that we get engaged and then married. She is our lifelong friend and the survival of our race depends on her. On her death, a man seeks another wife. Why denounce her, the one from whom even kings are born?"*

Guru Granth Sahib 473

In other words, women should be highly valued because men are so dependent on them.

Being a granthi is a position of responsibility in a gurdwara and it is open to both men and women.

WOMEN OF COURAGE

Sikh history and public life are still dominated by men. The only contributors to the Guru Granth Sahib were men. The holy brotherhood of the Khalsa in each gurdwara is presided over by men – the Panj Pyares.

Yet:

- Guru Nanak's first follower was his eldest sister, Nanake.

- The Gurus' wives and other women of courage have had a great effect on the religion.

- In 1699, Guru Gobind Singh's wife first added sugar to the amrit.

- Women, as well as men, can be a granthi and look after a Guru Granth Sahib.

- The Five Ks are worn by both women and men. In some Sikh groups, the turban, a symbol of spiritual equality, is worn by both women and men.

- In the marriage hymn [the Lavan], the human soul's relationship with God is said to be like that of the devoted wife submitting herself with joy to her husband.

OVER TO **YOU** ▶▶▶

1 Describe three of the beliefs about women that Guru Nanak did not want his new religion of Sikhism to share.

2 What does the word 'grihasth' mean and why was it an important idea to introduce into the new Sikh religion?

3 In what ways has Sikhism tried to show that it treats women with respect?

TAKE TIME TO THINK

Do you think that Sikhism treats women better than one other religion that you have studied – or not? Give one or two reasons for your answer – whatever it is.

WEALTH AND POVERTY

There are two stories about Guru Nanak which are usually told by Sikhs when they are discussing attitudes towards wealth:

MALIK BHAGO AND BHAI LALO

Malik Bhago was a rich and important man in the village where he lived. When Guru Nanak visited, Malik Bhago naturally thought that he would stay with him. Instead, he headed towards the shack where a very poor man, Bhai Lalo, lived.

Malik Bhago was deeply offended and made his feelings very plain to Guru Nanak. He ordered Guru Nanak to visit him to explain his behaviour. When Guru Nanak did so he told Malik Bhago that his food was impure. His bread was made with the blood of the people that he had exploited. On the other hand, Bhai Lalo's food was pure because it was made with the milk of honest work.

A *"He who eats what he earns through hard work and gives with his own hand, he alone knows the true way of life."*

Guru Nanak

Sikhism teaches that the poor need to be helped if their poverty is not their own fault.

DUNI CHAND

Every time Duni Chand made a 1,000,000 rupees, he flew a flag from his house. When Guru Nanak met him, there were several flags fluttering in the breeze. The Guru asked him to keep a needle for him and to let him have it back in the next life. Duni Chand was delighted to have been honoured by Guru Nanak's visit.

He ran all the way home to tell his wife of the honour. His wife laughed at him. She asked him whether the Guru had told him how to carry anything from this life to the next. She had watched many cremations and nothing seemed to survive the flames.

Duni Chand returned to Guru Nanak. Nanak told him that only faith and a reputation for good works lived on from one life to the next. For this reason, he had better put his trust in God and begin to serve his fellow human beings instead of exploiting them and cheating them out of their money.

Duni Chand became a Sikh, built a place of worship and began to take care of his neighbours.

SIKHS AND BEGGING

In the time of the Gurus, poor Hindu villagers had to work very hard until they died. There were no sickness benefits or retirement pensions in those days. They were despised by everyone, yet holy men would often beg from them. The Gurus taught that hard work was a way of serving God and something to be proud of, as long as it was honestly done.

For many Hindus at the time, and even today, begging was a profession. Sikhs disapprove of this. It does mean, however, that Sikhs must try to help beggars to find work of a kind that helps the society in which they live. For their own self respect, everyone needs to do this. Sikhs themselves should never beg.

Hard work and supporting those who depend on you is something that my parents have drummed into me since I was very young. They have always expected me to work hard at school and it is something that I now take for granted – and always will.

Virender, 18

TAKE TIME TO THINK

In some religions, people are encouraged to give away all, or much, of their wealth to help the poor. Do you think that Guru Nanak would approve of someone doing this? Give a reason or two for your answer.

OVER TO YOU ▶▶▶

Act out these two stories, trying to get inside the minds of the two main characters. Try to work out how Bhai Lalo felt when the Guru visited his home and how Duni Chand eventually saw sense. Discuss the part that Guru Nanak played in getting over his message to these two people.

LOOKING AFTER THE ELDERLY

You will find out

- The responsibility that all Sikhs feel towards the elderly.

- The importance of the gurdwara in looking after the elderly.

In the glossary

Gurdwara

Guru

Punjab

More and more gurdwaras are providing facilities to look after elderly people.

Improved hygiene and medical care has increased the number of elderly people in the Punjab and elsewhere. The same concern for the elderly is found, however, wherever there is a Sikh family.

WHOSE RESPONSIBILITY ARE THE ELDERLY?

Most Sikhs remember the warning which Guru Ram Das gave to his eldest son:

A *"It is the greatest sin to quarrel with parents who have given you birth and brought you up."*

Guru Granth Sahib 1200

All Sikhs are taught to have the greatest respect for their parents and to show them all the necessary love and attention. In particular, this duty to care for them falls on the shoulders of the sons in the family. This is why all Sikh parents are concerned that they should have male children.

When Asians began to settle in Western countries, they were very disturbed at the way that aged parents were put into old people's homes. They were fearful of the shame that they would suffer among other Asians if they used any of the services provided for the elderly.

The words of one of their respected leaders explain how important this respect is for most Sikhs:

B *"When a man acts in a morally irresponsible manner towards his parents his religious acts and worship are futile."*

Var 37.13

THE IMPORTANCE OF THE GURDWARA

Sikhs are beginning to realise that elderly people need more support and help in the modern world than the family alone can provide. The obvious way of doing this is through the gurdwara and these are beginning to provide:

CHECK IT OUT

A welcoming centre where the elderly can be helped and given the opportunity to talk among themselves.

An opportunity for Sikhs and non-Sikhs to learn about one another.

Increasingly, gurdwaras are providing:

An opportunity for Sikhs to carry out acts of service such as hoovering or preparing tea for the elderly.

A day-centre to counteract the loneliness and sense of isolation that so many older people feel.

A new venture was begun in the Punjab in 1958, where a home for the elderly was set up and funded by donations from Indian Sikhs. This has pointed the way forward in the future for the care of the elderly. Families in Asia and the West are finding it increasingly difficult to look after the elderly without some kind of support from elsewhere.

In the life of Guru Amar Das, Sikhs have a reminder that age need not lead to a lessening of service offered to the Sikh community. He was 73 when he became Guru and he served the community for 22 years!

TAKE TIME TO THINK

What do you think that Western countries could learn from the way that elderly people are respected in Sikhism?

OVER TO **YOU** ▶▶▶

If there is a Sikh gurdwara close to where you live, see if someone can visit you or maybe your class can visit them. This will give you the opportunity to find out many things about Sikhism, including the arrangements that it has for looking after the elderly members of the local community.

OR visit the following websites to find out the same information:
www.bbc.co.uk/religion/religions/sikhism/index.shtml
www.Sikhs.org
http://www.religionfacts.com/sikhism/index.htm

WHAT IS EUTHANASIA?

Euthanasia, also called 'mercy killing', means ending a person's life when all joy and pleasure has been replaced by pain and suffering. For someone to do this without a person's permission would be murder.

- What, though, if the person was to ask someone to do it?
- What if the person was too ill to do this?

The answers to these questions are rarely simple and straightforward. Should a person who is unconscious and without any hope of recovery, for example, be put on a life-support machine for a long time?

Sikhs believe that everything should be done to make the sick and elderly comfortable.

God's gift

Sikhs believe that all life is given by God. It may be happy or sad. It may be long or short. The length, and the nature, of a person's life is totally in the hands of God. Nobody has the right to shorten it by any act that they carry out. Here are two comments by Guru Nanak:

A *"God sends us and we take birth. God calls us back and we die."*

Guru Granth Sahib 1239

B *"Who knows how we shall come to die? Who knows what manner of death will be ours?"*

Guru Granth Sahib 555

Sikhs believe that everything is in God's hands and nobody should meddle with this – and that covers both suicide and euthanasia.

Euthanasia and the Sikh community

Sikhs in India have not had to make their minds up on such issues. Life support machines are only found in the largest hospitals and there is no way that a person's life can be ended early. What, though, would a Sikh bear in mind when making up his or her mind on the issue?

1. Giving loving care to the sufferer is the first consideration.

2. Any attempt to end a person's life early for financial reasons is completely immoral.

3. The Sikh belief about caring for the elderly or the incurably ill finds no place for deliberately ending their life early.

4. All Sikhs should accept what God sends as an expression of the divine will. This includes, as we will see in Unit 31, any suffering.

5. Sikhs should spend some time, particularly towards the end of their life, meditating on the real meaning of life. Each Sikh is taught:

C *"The dawn of a new day is the herald of a sunset, Earth is not your permanent home."*

Guru Granth Sahib 793

D *"Know the real purpose of being here and gather up the treasure under the guidance of the True Guru [the Guru Granth Sahib]. Make your mind God's home. If he abides with you undisturbed, you will not be reborn."*

Guru Granth Sahib 13

OVER TO YOU ▶▶▶

1 What does the word 'euthanasia' mean?

2 Write two sentences to sum up the belief that Sikhs hold about life and death.

3 In the end, why do Sikhs reject the idea of ending a person's life early?

TAKE TIME TO THINK

Do you think that you could accept the idea that everything in life – good and bad – has to be accepted because it is God's will? Perhaps you already do?

BODY MATTERS

Sikhs look upon their body as a temple which has been built by God and which they should look after with great care. Its natural state should be maintained and respected.

CARING FOR THE BODY

One of the Sikh ideals is to leave their hair uncut. To a non-Sikh, this might seem trivial and unimportant. After all, what could possibly be wrong in cutting your hair? Sikhs would reply that:

- The Sikh Gurus did not cut their hair.
- Uncut hair is the natural form for it to take.
- This is the way that God intended it to be.

Sikhs also do not:

CHECK IT OUT

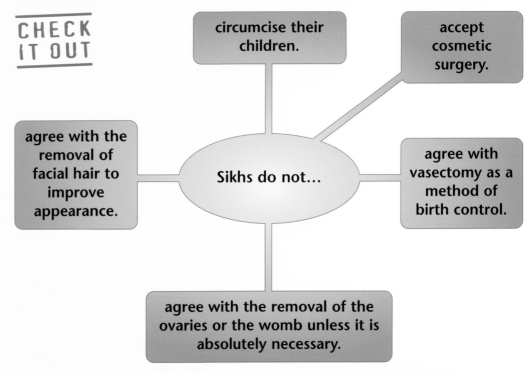

circumcise their children.

accept cosmetic surgery.

agree with the removal of facial hair to improve appearance.

Sikhs do not...

agree with vasectomy as a method of birth control.

agree with the removal of the ovaries or the womb unless it is absolutely necessary.

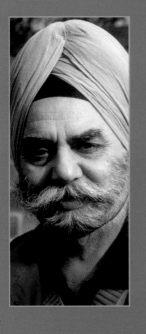

DRUGS

Smoking tobacco and taking drugs are both forbidden for Sikhs. Taking them clouds the mind, damages the lungs and heart, and makes the body unclean. They do accept, however, that drugs prescribed by a doctor are sometimes necessary.

In the day of Guru Nanak, it was quite normal for drugs to be used. When the Guru had an audience with the Emperor Babur, at a town called Saidpur – which had just been captured, he was offered a drink containing opium. He replied that he was "hooked" on praising God.

Drinking alcohol was condemned by the Gurus and is forbidden to Sikhs today:

A *"By drinking wine one loses sanity and becomes mad; one loses the power of discrimination and incurs God's displeasure."*

Guru Granth Sahib 554

and the Sikh Code of Discipline adds:

B *"Sikhs should not partake of alcohol, tobacco, drugs or any other intoxicants."*

A Sikh who smokes after being initiated into the Khalsa must undergo the initiation again. There is no better demonstration of how badly Sikhs view smoking than that.

The main reason why Sikhs wear turbans is so that their long hair can be kept neat and tidy.

TAKE TIME TO THINK

What do you think Sikhs mean when they say that cleanliness is the most important virtue next to godliness?

OVER TO **YOU** ▶▶▶

1 Sikhs maintain that uncut hair is a symbol of their identity as Sikhs. What do you think they mean when they say this?

2 Imagine that you are a Sikh boy or girl away from home at college and you decide to have your hair cut.
   a) Write a letter to your parents explaining the reasons for your decision.
   b) Compose a letter which might be written from your parents in return.

3 What is the main reason why Sikhism is opposed to the drinking of alcohol?

Sikhs accept that suffering is real but they hope that they can go beyond the suffering. To explain this, a Sikh points to the way, for example, that someone can forget their toothache if they are invited to a party.

A Sikh also points out that much suffering can be explained without a problem. There are, he believes, moral laws which carry consequences if they are broken. Breaking them has the same effect on young and old, rich and poor, the clever and the foolish. As Guru Nanak pointed out:

A *"Whoever tastes poison will die."*

Guru Granth Sahib 142

THE MYSTERY OF SUFFERING

There is, of course, a mystery why many things happen as they do and that includes much suffering. Guru Nanak taught:

B *"The more we find out the more there is still to discover."*

Guru Granth Sahib 5

There is much about suffering we will never understand. The Gurus taught that God, the Timeless Being, knows the reason behind much suffering but He has chosen not to tell us. We simply have to accept our fate:

C *"From the beginning of time pain and pleasure are written in humanity's fate by the Creator."*

Guru Granth Sahib 1054/18

Only God knows why some people suffer more than others.

FAITH CAN OVERCOME PAIN

Sikhs believe that people can become detached from their pain by:

- Contemplating the glory of God and
- Discovering the inner presence of God.

The better anyone knows God, the more willing they are to accept the will of God. As Guru Nanak advised them to say:

D *"Lord, when I am happy I will worship you only; when I suffer, I will not forget you."*

Guru Granth Sahib 757

The story is told of the fifth Guru, Guru Arjan Dev, when he was being tortured by soldiers of the Mughal emperor. A well known Muslim was allowed to see the Guru and offered to try to use his influence to help him. Guru Arjan Dev replied: "It is God's will and I am at peace with God's name on my lips."

The ninth Guru, Guru Tegh Bahadur, managed to face a cruel death in the same way.

Is anyone to blame for the condition of this person?

EVIL

Much suffering comes from the wrong choices that people make. Sikhs believe that all good and all evil come from God – the source of everything. Just as there are poisonous and life-giving plants, so there are evil and good choices to be made all the time. Human beings cannot blame God if they make the wrong choices.

Pride

Attachment

The five evils in life

Anger

Lust

Greed

OVER TO YOU ▶▶▶

1 a) Sikhs believe that there are five evils in life. Make your own list of as many evils in life as you can and explain why some of them seem to lead on to other evils as well. Compare your list with other people in class.

   b) Which do you think is the greatest evil of all?

2 Do you blame God when you suffer?

TAKE TIME TO THINK

Think of two examples of 'undeserved suffering'.

a) How do you think a Sikh might explain them?
b) How would you explain them?

SIKHISM AND MEDICAL SCIENCE

From its earliest history, Sikhism has always cared for the sick by building hospitals and dispensaries. In some of the stories of his life, Guru Nanak is described as healing lepers. Guru Arjan Dev is also said to have built a hospital for the care of lepers. Leprosy was considered to be a highly contagious disease at the time of the Gurus.

Today, many Sikhs work as doctors and nurses. India, however, cannot afford to employ many of them and it depends heavily on voluntary overseas help.

Here are three areas of medical science of interest to Sikhs in the modern world:

TRANSPLANT SURGERY

Blindness is a major problem in India. Sikhs are encouraged to donate their corneas on death so that these can be grafted to save the sight of others. Many Sikhs donate their kidneys, while others donate their whole bodies on death. This does not present any religious problems for a Sikh:

A *"The dead may be cremated or buried, or thrown to the dogs, or cast into the waters or down an empty well. No one knows where the soul goes and disappears to."*

Guru Granth Sahib 648

Sikhs believe that, once they have died, their body is no more use than that of a discarded skin to a lizard.

GENETIC ENGINEERING

This process involves changing the basic structure of human cells. It can prevent parents from handing on hereditary diseases to their children. Most Sikhs feel that this is tampering with something, the human body, that God has created. Even if the baby is handicapped, it has still been created by God and so should be lovingly cared for by its parents and family.

ARTIFICIAL INSEMINATION

This can take one of two forms:

- Fertilising the ovum of the woman with her husband's sperm outside her body. The fertilised egg is then implanted into her body to grow normally. Sikhs would see no objection to this. It is a case of science helping and increasing human happiness.

- Using the sperm of another man to fertilise the woman's ovum because her husband is infertile. Sikh teachings believe that this is morally wrong. This would be the same as adultery. The only acceptable alternative if a couple are infertile is for the couple to adopt a baby or to remain childless.

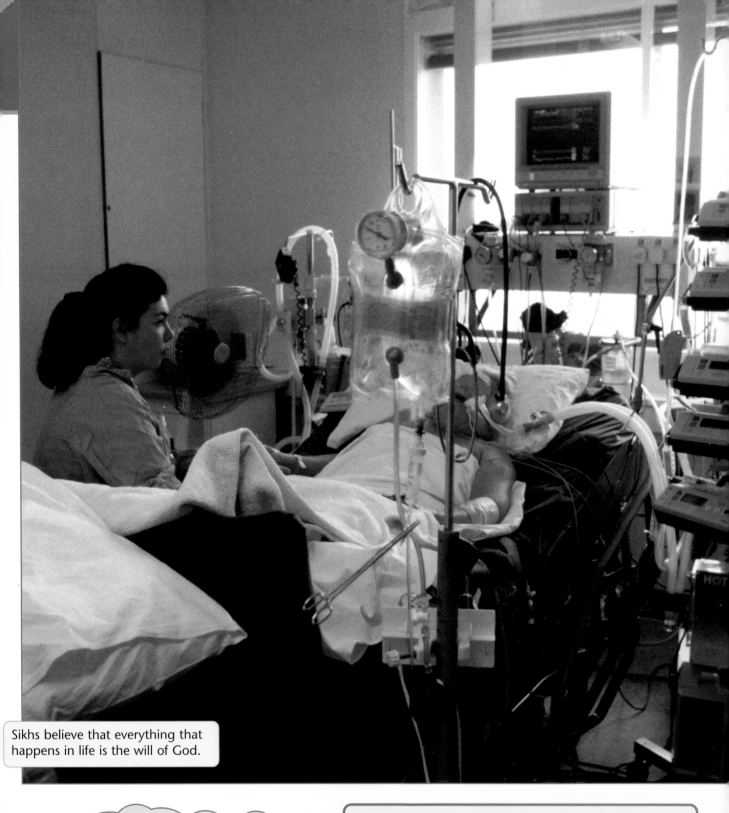

Sikhs believe that everything that happens in life is the will of God.

TAKE TIME TO THINK

Many people who are not Sikhs, or even religious, feel unhappy about scientists tinkering with the human body. Do you think it would be a good thing if all handicaps could be removed before a baby is born? Why might someone object to this?

OVER TO **YOU** ▶▶▶

1 Why are Sikhs happy for any organ to be transplanted from one person to another.

2 Explain why a Sikh would be unhappy with genetic engineering.

3 a) What are the two basic forms that artificial insemination can take?

  b) Why would a Sikh be happy with one of these forms but not the other?

GLOSSARY

Adi Granth: The Sikh scriptures before it became the last Guru of the Sikhs.

Akhand Path: The uninterrupted reading of the Guru Granth Sahib.

Amrit: Word used to describe the holy water, made by dissolving sugar crystals, used in many Sikh ceremonies.

Amrit-Dhari: A Sikh man or woman who has undertaken the initiation ceremony and undergone a form of baptism to become a member of the Khalsa.

Amrit Pahul: The initiation service into membership of the Khalsa carried out by the five Panj Pyares.

Amritsar: The holy town of Sikhism built by Guru Ram Das in 1576.

Anand Karaj: The Sikh wedding service.

Ardas: The most important Sikh prayer, recited in most Sikh religious ceremonies.

Chauri: A fan traditionally made of yak's hair which is waved by the granthi over the Guru Granth Sahib in a gurdwara.

Dasam Granth: Sikh scriptures thought to have been written, in the main, by Guru Gobind Singh.

Euthanasia: The practice of easing someone's death when they have an incurable illness.

Five Ks: The five symbols worn by members of the Khalsa.

Golden Temple: The holiest temple in Sikhism, in Amritsar, covered with gold leaf.

Granthi: Man or woman who is given responsibility of looking after the Guru Granth Sahib while it is in the gurdwara.

Grihasth: A householder, one of the four stages of life in Hinduism.

Gurdwara: 'The doorway to the Guru', the Sikh place of worship, which must contain a copy of the Guru Granth Sahib.

Gurmukhi: 'Proceeding from the mouth of the Guru', the language in which the Guru Granth Sahib is written.

Guru: A spiritual teacher, someone who is a spiritual instructor and leads others to the truth.

Guru Gobind Singh: The last human Sikh Guru.

Guru Granth Sahib: The Holy Scriptures of Sikhism, the last Guru after the death of Guru Gobind Singh.

Guru Nanak: The first Guru and the founder of Sikhism.

Gutka: A shortened form of the Guru Granth Sahib, used by most Sikhs in their devotions.

Harimandir: The building that is affectionately known by Sikhs as the Golden Temple in Amritsar.

Hukam: The random reading of a portion from the Guru Granth Sahib that is part of most Sikh services and ceremonies.

Infanticide: The ancient practice of killing baby girls at birth.

Japji: The opening hymn or chapter of the Guru Granth Sahib, written by Guru Nanak.

Kachs: Traditional baggy underpants worn by members of the Khalsa.

Kangha: A small wooden comb, one of the five symbols of the Khalsa.

Kara: A steel bracelet worn on the right wrist, one of the five symbols of the Khalsa.

Karah Parshad: Sweet food offered to those attending worship in a gurdwara.

Karma: The law of cause and effect which controls rebirth, a person's next birth being determined by previous lives.

Kesh: One of the five symbols of the Khalsa, it is forbidden for members to cut their hair.

Khalsa: The Sikh brotherhood initiated by Guru Gobind Singh in 1699, open to both male and female Sikhs.

Khanda: The double-edged sword symbolising spiritual authority, the supreme symbol of the Khalsa.

Kirpan: A short, curved knife, one of the five symbols of the Khalsa.

Langar: 'The Guru's Kitchen', free kitchen attached to every gurdwara, where meals are cooked during services.

Lavan: Name given to four verses in the Guru Granth Sahib composed by Guru Ram Das and used as a wedding hymn.

Moksha: The final release of the soul from the almost endless cycle of rebirth.

Mool Mantra: The first few lines of the Japji, written by Guru Nanak, forms the opening of the Guru Granth Sahib.

Nam: The Sikh name for God.

Nishan Sahib: The Sikh flag which is always flown outside a gurdwara.

Nit-Nem: The daily recitation of prayers taken from the Guru Granth Sahib.

Panj Pyares: The five Sikhs who responded to the call of Guru Gobind Singh and became the founder members of the Khalsa.

Patka: The small turban worn by Sikh boys until they are old enough to wear the full turban.

Punjab: The area in which Sikhism was born and where the vast majority of Sikhs are still found.

Rahiras: An important Sikh prayer.

Reincarnation: Belief held by Sikhs and Hindus that the soul is reborn many times before it reaches moksha.

Romala: Silk cloth used to cover the Guru Granth Sahib in the gurdwara when it is not being used.

Sati: The outlawed practice of widows throwing themselves on the burning funeral pyres of their husbands.

Simran: The continuous remembrance of God which, according to the teachings of the Gurus, is achieved through a continuous repetition of God's name.

Takht: The throne on which the Guru Granth Sahib sits in a gurdwara.

Turban: Head covering worn by male Sikhs, to catch up their long hair and keep it tidy.

Waheguru: A common exclamation of faith in the Gurus and their teachings, meaning 'Wonderful Lord'.

Badger Publishing Limited
15 Wedgwood Gate
Pin Green Industrial Estate
Stevenage, Hertfordshire SG1 4SU
Telephone: 01438 356907
Fax: 01438 747015
www.badger-publishing.co.uk
enquiries@badger-publishing.co.uk

Badger KS3 Religious Education
Sikh Beliefs and Issues

First published 2007
ISBN 978-1-84691-089 0

Text © Michael Keene 2007
Complete work © Badger Publishing Limited 2007

Acknowledgements
Photos © Alex Keene, The Walking Camera, with the following exceptions:
7 © World Religions Photo Library; 19 © Eye Ubiquitous;
22 © Sally and Richard Greenhill; 23 © Tom Allwood; 30 © Bubbles Photolibrary;
32 © David Grossman / Alamy.
21, 29 © Eye Ubiquitous / Hutchison.
33 © Shout / Rex Features.

Publisher: David Jamieson
Editor: Paul Martin
Designer: Adam Wilmott
Cover photo: Alex Keene, The Walking Camera

Printed in Hong Kong through Colorcraft Ltd.